T0195835

Hanna Fett

The Shepherd's Promises

Changing your life praying Psalm 23

WestBow Press books may be ordered through booksellers or by contacting:

WestBow Press
A Division of Thomas Nelson & Zondervan
1663 Liberty Drive
Bloomington, IN 47403
www.westbowpress.com
844-714-3454

Because of the dynamic nature of the Internet, any web addresses or links contained in this book may have changed since publication and may no longer be valid. The views expressed in this work are solely those of the author and do not necessarily reflect the views of the publisher, and the publisher hereby disclaims any responsibility for them.

NKJV:
Scripture taken from the New King James Version® Copyright © 1982 by Thomas Nelson. Used by permission. All rights reserved.

ISBN: 978-1-6642-6584-4 (sc)
ISBN: 978-1-6642-6585-1 (e)

Library of Congress Control Number: 2022908332

Print information available on the last page.

WestBow Press rev. date: 08/18/2022

WESTBOW
PRESS®
A DIVISION OF THOMAS NELSON
& ZONDERVAN

Contents

Psalm 23

A Psalm of David.

The LORD is my shepherd;
I shall not want.
He makes me to lie down in green pastures;
He leads me beside the still waters.
He restores my soul;
He leads me in the paths of righteousness
For His name's sake.

Yea, though I walk through the valley of the shadow of death,
I will fear no evil;
For You are with me;
Your rod and Your staff, they comfort me.

You prepare a table before me in the presence of my enemies;
You anoint my head with oil;
My cup runs over.
Surely goodness and mercy shall follow me
All the days of my life;
And I will dwell in the house of the LORD
Forever.

Preface

The notion of a higher being who protects, shelters, leads, guides, and watches over us is a desire found in most every human heart. Whether acknowledged or not, it is the soundless cry for God. Humanity longs to encounter a living God. The first three words of Psalm 23 assure His existence: "the Lord is." There is no beginning or end to this God. He is Alpha and Omega. He is ever present. And He is Lord—Lord of heaven and earth who has authority and power over all creation. And yet He is a God who deeply loves and cares for His creation. The words about this God, penned by David more than three thousand years ago, have brought more comfort and peace for people throughout the ages than any other passage of scripture.

There are many imageries David could have used to describe this God. Interestingly, he used the imagery of a shepherd. Having been a shepherd himself, David knew the attributes and characteristics of a good shepherd. They came alive as he experienced God in the hills near Bethlehem where he tended his father's sheep. It is there that David developed a personal, intimate relationship with God. Reflecting on his interactions and experiences with Him, David realizes that God is like a good shepherd who deeply cares for him. The Shepherd watches over him, leads and guides, protects and keeps him. David cannot but praise God. He longs to forever be in the presence of this God.

This psalm contains rich promises for anyone who turns by faith to the Lord Jesus Christ. It is my prayer that as you read through this psalm and prayerfully meditate on each verse, you would discover the depths of the wonderful promises of God as your personal shepherd.

Anointed worship music sets the atmosphere for the presence of God. It takes a worshipper with his or her heart and ear in tune with the Lord to capture heavenly inspired music. The music of Mark Payne flows from an intimate relationship with the Lord. Many prophets prophesied about a new sound being released by God. Mark Payne has captured the sounds of heaven to lead you into the presence of God.

Please scan the QR code or visit www.praypsalm23.com and enjoy the music from this renowned pianist and passionate worshipper.

There are times and seasons when the heart is heavy and there is just enough strength to lean on the prayer of a friend. For moments like these, we have recorded the prayer for you. Please visit www. praypsalm23.com or scan the QR code.

The Power of Declaring and Praying the Word of God

The Lord promises that His word shall not return void (Isa. 55:11). The implications of this promise are life changing because almighty God is assuring the fulfillment of His word. His word creates realities. How did Jesus heal the sick? How did He calm the storm or raise the dead? He spoke. Jesus used faith-filled words, knowing that His words have creative power, and He encouraged His followers to do the same. Mark 11:23 states that you can speak to a mountain and tell it to move, and if you believe, the mountain will move. Speaking God's Word in faith will bring results. Our words matter (Prov. 18:21). They have the power to bring transformation into our lives individually and kingdom reality into this world.

Using His Word as part of our prayer makes our prayers effective. We read in James 5:16 that the effective, fervent prayer of the righteous avails much. Praying, decreeing, and declaring God's Word will bring into our lives and this world what has already been established in heaven.

In Psalm 23, God reveals Himself as a Shepherd who cares for His sheep with deep love. Every verse contains a powerful truth about the character and nature of God. The corresponding prayer for each verse is based on scripture verses that confirm and support the manifold expression of God as Shepherd. As you speak His Word and declare who He is and what He does, He will manifest Himself to you. He promised that as you decree a thing, it shall be established for you (Job 22:28). As you pray through Psalm 23, expect God to reveal Himself to you as your good Shepherd who protects, provides, guides, restores, heals, leads, anoints, and loves you with an unfailing love.

The following prayers are based on scripture. They are not direct quotations from the Bible, but these are paraphrased confessions based on the scripture under each prayer.

5

The Lord Is My Shepherd

You are Lord. You are not just a god but Lord of lords and King of kings. You are God Almighty, creator of heaven and earth, Alpha and Omega, beginning and end. One day, at Your name, every knee will bow and every tongue will confess that You are Lord. Your existence is undeniable. You are. You are ever present, never changing. You are always there for me, for Your promise is true; as I draw near to You, You draw near to me.

You, O Lord and King, are my shepherd. You know my name and everything about me. You even know the number of hairs on my head. Thank You for being a personal God who tenderly cares for me. You watch over me and protect me. Fear shall not come near me. You, O Lord, are my refuge, my strong tower, my safe haven. Nothing and nobody is more powerful than You are. You fight my battles. Thank You for the authority You have given me. In Your name I can defeat any evil spirits coming against me so I can live in peace and freedom.

If I walk away from You, You seek me. You chase after me just to take me into Your arms and bring me back to a place of safety and communion with You. I am never alone because You are always with me. I am so grateful for Your promise to never leave me nor forsake me. There is nothing that can separate me from Your wonderful love. I am Yours.

You make me part of a family. By Your spirit, I am one with You and with other believers. Jesus, You say You are the good Shepherd who knows His sheep and gives them eternal life. You promise that I shall not perish and that no one can snatch me out of Your hand. I am safe with You. Thank You, Jesus, for being my good Shepherd who has willingly laid down His life for me. I gladly listen to You and follow You.

(Revelation 17:14; Revelation 22:13; Genesis 14:19; Psalm 115:15; Philippians 2:10–11; Exodus 3:14; James 4:8; Exodus 33:17; Luke 12:7; Isaiah 41:10; Isaiah 41:13; Proverbs 8:10; Deuteronomy 31:6; Romans 8:38–39; Psalm 68:6; John 3:16; John 10:28)

I Shall Not Want

Because You are everything, I shall not want for anything. Your nature, O Lord, is to bless and give. Everything You have, Jesus, You give to me. You make me a coheir. You have blessed me with every spiritual blessing in the heavenlies. You promised that You would not withhold any good thing from those who walk blameless. Every good and perfect gift comes from You. Daily You load me up with good things I can benefit from. Every day I have the privilege to enjoy Your goodness.

I shall not lack provision and resources because You promised that I will have sufficiency for every good work. You are El Shaddai, my provider. You, O Lord, bless abundantly above all I can ever ask or think. Every day You lavish Your blessings upon me. Your blessings satisfy. They empower me to be prosperous.

I shall not want for love because Your love never fails me. I shall not lack for friends and fellowship because You, Jesus, stick closer than a brother. Whenever I turn toward You, You turn toward me. Every time. You embrace me with the open arms of a Father.

Thank You, Lord; I shall never lack for peace because You give peace beyond understanding, no matter what my circumstances are telling me.

I shall not lack for joy because in Your presence is fullness of joy. When I think about who You are, joy fills my heart because nothing is impossible with You. You alone, Lord, satisfy my soul.

I shall not want for health because You are Jehovah Rapha, the God who heals. By Your stripes, I am healed. With the authority You have given me, Jesus, I speak health into my body and healing to my soul.

I shall not want for purpose and destiny because You have good thoughts toward me You give me a future and a hope. You invite me to colabor with You. What a privilege to join You in Your work here on earth. Thank You, Lord; I shall not want for anything.

(Romans 8:16–17; Ephesians 1:3; Psalm 84:11; James 1:17; Psalm 68:19; Corinthians 9:8; Ephesians 3:20–21, Proverbs 18:24; James 4:8; Hebrews 4:16; Philippians 4:7; Psalm 16:11; Matthew 19:26; Isaiah 53:5; Jeremiah 29:11; 1 Corinthians 3:9)

He Makes Me Lie Down in Green Pastures

Like a shepherd leading sheep to green pastures, You guide me into a place of safety and prosperity. You have abundance for me. Jesus, You came to give me life, and life more abundantly. Wherever You lead me, there is always a place of rest in You. I can rest in Your luxurious love and enjoy Your perfect provision. In the bliss of Your presence, my restless soul finds peace. I let go of strife and worry. I don't have to work for Your favor or love. I can cease from my works and receive like a child receiving from a Father.

Because of You, Jesus, I am in right standing with the Father. I am righteous in You, justified and free from the effects of sin and death. I am holy and without blame before You. I am complete in You. Perfect harmony of You and me. In You, O Lord, I put my trust. I trust You with my life because no matter what I go through, You let all things work together for good. Thank You, Lord, for You have given me all things to enjoy. You make me lie down in green pastures.

(John 10:10; 2 Corinthians 5:21; Romans 8:28; 1 Timothy 6:17)

He leads me besides Still waters

Thank You, Lord, for being so gentle as You lead me. Whenever I feel like I am in a dry place with You, I know You will not leave me there. You lead me into Your presence. What a beautiful, quiet place to be still and know that You are God. My soul rests in You. I know I can totally trust You with my life. All that is burdensome to me, I lay down at Your feet. I give You my disappointments, discouragement, and weaknesses. Let Your peace flood my soul. Overwhelm me with Your goodness, Lord. You alone, Lord, can calm my restless mind, drowning my worries and fear in Your endless love.

I love Your presence, Lord. I come alive again because You are the source of life. You renew my vision, giving me purpose and destiny. Yet again, You instill hope, shalom peace, and joy unspeakable within me. You refresh my soul.

Thank You for being so willing to pour out Your Holy Spirit. I embrace You, Holy Spirit. Come and fill me yet again so that streams of living water flow from me. Anywhere I go, anyone I meet, let Your holy presence be manifested. Let Your Spirit flow from me to others so we all have the opportunity to taste and see that You are a good God. You invite anyone who is thirsty to come and drink. Freely You give. Whoever tastes of the water You give will never thirst again. You satisfy the soul. You give more than enough—not just sufficiency but abundance. Fill me to overflowing with Your Holy Spirit, and bless me so I can be a blessing.

(Psalm 46:10; 1 Peter 1:8; John 7:38; Psalm 34:8; Matthew 11:28; John 4:14; Isaiah 58:11)

He Restores My Soul

Lord, You are a God of restoration. You embrace me with grace and loving-kindness. My soul is safe with You. Your deep and unconditional love is like pure liquid, flowing through my innermost being and gently healing my wounded heart. Your acceptance and love are healing to me. You heal the hurts caused by rejection. Your acceptance of me turns my insecurities into confidence. Every fear and even the smallest doubts disappear in the presence of Your love. Your love covers me. You give me beauty for ashes and make me beautiful. Whatever has been hurt, destroyed, and died in me, You restore again. Thank You, Jesus, for transforming me into Your likeness. Today I grow in the knowledge of who You are. Thank You for being faithful to complete the work that You have begun. You restore my mind, will, and emotions so I can live a life pleasing to You, filled with love, joy, peace, and purpose.

Thank You, Jesus, for giving me the mind of Christ. I declare that today I think God thoughts and decree kingdom realities. Lord, give me Your wisdom for every situation I face today and every decision I must make. I decree and declare that I will not judge by what I see with my eyes but follow Your voice in obedience. I choose to be obedient to You, Lord.

Lord, I align my will with Your will. Let Your will be done, Your kingdom come, on earth as it is in heaven, in my life and through my life. I submit myself to You. I decree and declare that I will fulfill all the purposes of God.

Lord, You promised to heal the broken-hearted. I give You every emotional hurt and pain. Saturate me with Your love. Let Your love invade my innermost being and gently heal my wounded heart. Lavish Your healing balm on the wounds that careless words have left in my heart. Drown the pain from feeling betrayed and rejected in Your deep love. Thank You, Lord, for restoring my soul.

(Psalm 147:3; Isaiah 61:1; 1 John 4:18; 2 Corinthians 3:18; Philippians 1:6; 1 Corinthians 2:16; Psalm 147:3)

He Guides Me
in the Paths of Righteousness
for His Name's Sake

Jesus, You said narrow is the path that leads into Your kingdom. Thank You, Jesus, for guiding me. Like a shepherd watching out for his sheep, You watch out for me. I trust You with my life, one day at a time. With Your gentle voice, You whisper to my spirit and direct my footsteps. Help me not to judge by sight, but infuse my heart with kingdom truth. Give me grace and help me to change, progress, and develop a kingdom mentality. Let me think kingdom thoughts and act accordingly. In areas where You have revealed Your will for me through Your Word, give me grace to walk in obedience to Your Word. Where I am free to decide and many options look good to me, give me Your counsel.

Thank You, Lord, for allowing me to know that everything I encounter in life serves Your purpose because You work all things together for my good. Jesus, You paid the price for me to be in right standing with God. I am so grateful for my relationship with You. Knowing You is my heart's desire. Give me grace to walk out Your will and desires in my life. You know all about my abilities, potentials, shortcomings, and limitations. You know exactly how to gently lead me. You are faithful and dependable. No circumstance takes You by surprise. But You are well able to keep me on the right path, a path that leads to the full revelation of who You are. Thank You for Your promise that the light shines ever brighter till the full light of day. Today's light is brighter than yesterday's, and tomorrow's will be brighter than today's. Thank You, Lord, that my future is bright. Help me today to will and to do for Your good pleasure; let my will and all I do cause You joy. Let my life reflect Your glory for Your name's sake.

(Matthew 7:13; Proverbs 3:5–6; Romans 8:28; 2 Corinthians 5:21; Proverbs 4:18; Philippians 2:13)

Though I Walk Through the Valley
of the Shadow of Death,
I Will Fear No Evil,
for You Are
With Me

There are days when I am struggling, when I feel overwhelmed, discouraged, hurt, and lonely. Jesus, You are familiar with every emotion and every thought I have. There is nothing that You have not walked through. Lord, I find great comfort in knowing that I can freely share my innermost, deepest feelings and thoughts with You. For You are my closest friend who listens and cares. You say You will stick closer than a brother, and You do. You are there, even when I don't feel You. As fear wells up in me, I turn to You. Saturate me afresh with Your perfect love that casts out all fear. Knowing that I am loved and cared for by You, almighty God, gives me peace. Cover my vulnerability with Your presence. Nothing can bully me into fear because Your promise stands: no weapon formed against me shall prosper. I put my faith in You.

Right now, I can't see what lies ahead, but I trust You, my Shepherd. You are leading me through this dark season. The only way forward is going through it as You fight my battles, because the battles and vengeance belong to You. Thank You, Lord, for not allowing difficulty, pain, loss, and disappointment to be my final destination but just seasons that will pass. I will walk through situations and circumstances that seem like a deep, dark shadow of a death-like valley. I will walk through and come out of the valley. As I walk through the valley, You are my protector, keeping me safe. Thank You, Lord, that my life is not a dead-end street. I am passing through the valleys I cannot avoid with You on my side. You are my light in my darkest moments. You give hope when I feel like giving up. You gently wipe away my tears with Your love. Thank You for not making me walk alone. Thank You for sending people along the path to walk with me. I decree and declare that I will fear no evil, for You are with me, Jesus.

(Proverbs 18:24; 1 John 4:18; Isaiah 54:17; 2 Chronicles 20:15; Romans 12:19; Psalm 46:7)

Your Rod and your Staff,
They Comfort Me

Thank You, Lord, for Your guidance today. Like a shepherd using his rod to keep the sheep on the right track, keep me today on the right path. Speak to me through Your Word to correct any thoughts, words, and deeds not pleasing to You. Keep me from any temptation. Thank You for helping me navigate through this day. Like a shepherd using his staff for support, I lean on You for support and strength. You promised to be my strength and an ever-present help in times of trouble. Thank You for being absolute and unfailingly dependable.

Holy Spirit, I welcome You in my life. You are my comforter. You remind me of who God is and what He can do when life throws me a curveball. I love it when Your Holy Spirit whispers in my ear, reminding me of all the times You have faithfully helped me. When finances are tight, You remind me of the provisional miracles You did for me. When I don't see a way out, You remind me of the many doors You have opened for me. What an exciting journey it has been so far to walk with You, Jesus. Every time You manifested Yourself to me, You revealed a part of who You are: You are my provider. You are my healer. You are my waymaker. You are my peace in the storm. You are my miracle worker. I choose to focus on You. I choose to believe Your Word and Your promises. I choose to trust in You. Like David, I know—I will yet praise You.

(John 10:27; Psalm 41:1; 1 Thessalonians 3:3; Revelation 3:8; Psalm 42:11)

You Prepare a Table before Me
in the Presence of My Enemies

No matter what goes on around me, even if I am surrounded by people who try to cause me harm, You satisfy me with good things. You prepare, organize, and order circumstances to ultimately be a blessing because You promised all things work together for good for those who love You. You invite me to sit with You and dine with You. You treat me to a lavish feast. When my heart hungers for love, You are there to love on me. When my soul thirsts for peace of mind, You breathe Your Holy Spirit on me to give me peace that passes understanding. When I am weary from the battles in life, You refresh my soul. You provide everything for me to live in liberty. You set me free from being bound, distressed, emotionally confined, and mentally troubled. At Your table, and in Your presence, I find liberty and restoration. Today, Lord, I feast on Your goodness. I drink the wine of forgiveness and eat the bread of healing. As I feast on You, restore and transform me. Lord, let me become a testimony to Your glory.

(Psalm 103:4–5; Psalm 103:6; Philippians 4:7)

You Anoint my Head with Oil

Thank You, Jesus, for dying on the cross for me. At incalculable cost, You made me worthy to be anointed with oil. Thank You for laying down Your life for me. What an honor to give my life back to You. I consecrate myself to You. I am Yours. Thank You for putting Your seal upon me. Today, pour out Your Holy Spirit upon me afresh, and anoint my head with oil so I can serve and represent You well today. You have chosen me and made me royalty. I receive everything I need to fulfill my calling. I am so grateful that despite my failures, You use me for Your glory.

Let Your anointing oil flow from the top of my head to the bottom of my feet. Let me smell Your fragrance and always remember You as I go through this day. Thank You for Your anointing oil that is like a barrier of protection against any evil thoughts that are trying to enter my mind. I take every thought captive that rises up against You. Any worrisome thought that tries to enter my mind cannot enter because You have given me the mind of Christ. Keep evil from me that tries to kill, steal, and destroy my happiness. Thank You for giving me spiritual authority to bind principalities and powers and every evil thing that would try to harm me. Your anointing oil also brings healing. Thank You for divine health and healing today. Thank You, Lord, for giving me the oil of gladness. You turn my sadness into joy. I praise and worship You, Lord Jesus.

(Psalm 103:4–5; Psalm 103:6; Philippians 4:7)

My Cup Runs Over

Whatever You do, Lord, You do exceedingly and abundantly above all I could ever ask or think. You are a God of superabundance. You give joy indescribable, peace that passes human understanding, life abundantly, and Your spirit without measure. Nothing is impossible with You. When I lay hands on the sick, they shall recover. When I speak Your Word, You do signs, wonders, and miracles. Thank You for the authority You have given me to bind and loose things in the spiritual realm so Your kingdom reality can manifest here on earth as it is in heaven. Thank You for allowing the same Holy Spirit that raised Jesus from the dead to be within me. Through You, Lord, I have power and authority to raise the dead and to come against tormenting spirits. Freely You give of Your Holy Spirit, so I can freely give to others.

You bless, so I can be a blessing. You are so generous. When I give anything to You or in Your name to others, it shall be given to me pressed down, shaken together, and running over. Lord, I cannot outgive You. You always give back more than I can imagine. You are so willing to bless because You want the best for me. There is always provision for me. My cup runs over.

(Ephesians 3:20; Psalm 16:11; Philippians 4:6; John 10:10; John 3:34; Luke 1:37; Mark 16:17–18; Matthew 18:18; Romans 8:11; Luke 6:38)

Surely Goodness and Mercy
Shall Follow Me
All the Days of My Life

Thank You for Your faithfulness, Lord. You keep all Your promises. Not maybe or sometimes, but surely goodness and mercy shall follow me. Thank You, Lord, for Your loyal, irrevocable covenant love. Your goodness and mercy are pursuing me today. When I become weary, Your steadfast love spurs me on, driving me closer to Jesus. Today, draw me closer to You, and give me a deeper understanding of who You are. It is Your goodness, Lord, that leads me to change my ways. I want to please You today. Steer me in the right direction today, and keep evil from me. Bless me and bless me indeed.

As I look back, my life bears evidence of Your goodness and mercy. With great love and compassion, You have picked me up when I have fallen. I am so grateful that You never give up on me. Lord, You are so quick to forgive, so willing to draw me close to You again and again. Whatever the trial, Your loving-kindness follows me. Every day of my life, I can expect Your blessing. It is Your pleasure to bless with acts of mercy, grace, and love. Thank You, Jesus, for manifesting Your goodness and mercy in my life today.

(1 Corinthians 1:9; Psalm 145:9; 1 Corinthians 16:34; 1 John 1:9)

And I Will Dwell in
The House of The Lord
Forever.

Thank You, Lord, for giving me purpose and destiny. I know my final destination is to be in Your presence, seeing You face-to-face. Therefore, I will run this race, not looking back at what was yesterday. I will forget the things that are behind, and I press on to reach the end of the race and receive the heavenly prize for which You, Jesus, are calling. I will set my face like a flint and follow You because there is more to this life than meets the eye. There is a greater reality. Although I see heaven on earth sometimes manifest on this side of heaven, one day I will be fully immersed in it. The outcome of my life is secure. I will be with You forever.

For this purpose, I have been redeemed to live with You in eternal glory. I will enter Your gates with thanksgiving and Your courts with praise. I will live in Your house, not as a stranger but as Your child, joining in with the angels to worship You. Thank You, Jesus, for preparing a home for me in heaven. What a privilege and joy to one day finally be with You, immersed in Your presence, living in Your kingdom forever. My heart overflows with praise and adoration for You, O Lord, my Shepherd.

(1 Corinthians 13:12; Philippians 3:13–14; Romans 8:17; Psalm 100:4)

Bible Verses

Each prayer is based on the following Bible verses:

The Lord Is My Shepherd

Revelation 17:14
Revelation 22:13
Genesis 14:19
Psalm 115:15
Philippians 2:10–11
Exodus 3:14
James 4:8
Exodus 33:17
Luke 12:7
Isaiah 41:10
Isaiah 41:13
Proverbs 8:10
Deuteronomy 31:6
Romans 8:38–39
Psalm 68:6
John 3:16
John 10:28

I Shall Not Want

Romans 8:16–17
Ephesians 1:3
Psalm 84:11
James 1:17
Psalm 68:19
2 Corinthians 9:8
Ephesians 3:20–21
Proverbs 18:24
James 4:8
Hebrews 4:16
Philippians 4:7
Psalm 16:11
Matthew 19:26
Isaiah 53:5
Jeremiah 29:11
1 Corinthians 3:9

He Makes Me Lie Down in Green Pastures

John 10:10
2 Corinthians 5:21
Romans 8:28
1 Timothy 6:17

He Leads Me beside Still Waters

Psalm 46:10
1 Peter 1:8
John 7:38
Psalm 34:8
Matthew 11:28
John 4:14
Isaiah 58:11

He Restores My Soul

Psalm 147:3
Isaiah 61:1
1 John 4:18
2 Corinthians 3:18
Philippians 1:6
1 Corinthians 2:16
Psalm 147:3

He Guides Me in the Paths of Righteousness for His Name's Sake

Matthew 7:13
Proverbs 3:5–6
Romans 8:28
2 Corinthians 5:21
Proverbs 4:18
Philippians 2:13

Though I Walk through the Valley of the Shadow of Death, I Will Fear No Evil for You Are with Me

Proverbs 18:24
1 John 4:18
Isaiah 54:17
2 Chronicles 20:15
Romans 12:19
Psalm 46:7

Your Rod and Your Staff They Comfort Me

John 10:27
Psalm 41:1
1 Thessalonians 3:3
Revelation 3:8
Psalm 42:11

You Prepare a Table before Me in the Presence of My Enemies

Psalm 103:4–5
Psalm 103:6
Philippians 4:7

You Anoint My Head with Oil

Joel 2:28–29
2 Corinthians 1:21–22
Ephesians 1:13–14
1 Peter 2:9
2 Corinthians 10:4–5
John 10:10
Matthew 10:10

My Cup Runs Over

Ephesians 3:20
Psalm 16:11
Philippians 4:6
John 10:10
John 3:34 (NIV)
Luke 1:37
Mark 16:17–18
Matthew 18:18
Romans 8:11
Luke 6:38

Surely Goodness and Mercy Shall Follow Me All the Days of My Life

1 Corinthians 1:9
Psalm 145:9
1 Corinthians 16:34
1 John 1:9

And I Will Dwell in the House of the Lord Forever

1 Corinthians 13:12
Philippians 3:13–14
Romans 8:17
Psalm 100:4

Printed in the United States
by Baker & Taylor Publisher Services